Gotcha!

Gotcha!

Your little black book to a safer e-xperience

by Dr. Sally Ernst

Consulting Editor, Troy Braban

Copyright

Copyright © 2015 Dr. Sally Ernst
Consulting Editor, Troy Braban

In accordance with the U.S. Copyright Act of 1976 and the Australian Copyright Act 1968, the scanning, uploading, and electronic sharing of any part of this book without the permission of the publisher constitutes unlawful piracy and theft of the author's intellectual property. If you would like to use material from this book (other than for review purposes), prior written permission must be obtained by contacting the publisher at **info@goko.com.au**. Thank you for your support of the author's rights.

GOKO Publishing
PO Box 7109
McMahons Point 2060
Sydney. Australia
www.gokopublishing.com.au
First Edition 2015

Library of Congress Cataloguing-in-Publication Data

Ernst. Dr. Sally
    GOTCHA! Your little black book to a safer e-xperience
    p. cm.
ISBN: 978-1613398081
LCCN: 2015909375

Book Designed by Katherine Owen
Printed in Australia

Foreword
by Troy Braban

I met Sally a few years back through an introduction from a mutual friend. Our mutual friend suspected that we would enjoy the discussion given our similar passion for cyber security, education, empowering boards and directors, and the work that we do. I personally enjoyed the discussion and Sally and I are now "collaborators", enthused by making a contribution back to our industry. Sally is passionate, curious, dedicated and a little crazy because she is willing to tackle something far larger than many would even contemplate: how one person can connect with a range of networks to change an industry. This is a great mission, something in which I am convinced Sally will succeed.

This book is one such passion. I remember when Sally first shared with me about many of her discussions with directors, senior executives and even board members who were interested in this thing called cyber security but did not really know where to start. In her own research she found such a large array of confusing and overwhelming information, ranging from deeply technical to deeply wrong.

The idea for this book was pitched perfectly to me when Sally described it saying, "I want a board member to buy this book at the airport bookshop and read it cover to cover on a short plane flight. At the end of that flight, they'll have a deeper understanding of cyber security and be armed with insight and questions for their

next discussion". This is a great objective and if the book hits this goal, it will have made a positive and impactful contribution to the industry. I believe it can and will, which is why I am pleased to write this foreword.

I have been lucky enough to look after cyber security at a couple of different organisations. In each case I have loved the interaction with our board and our senior executives. Education is important, but moving from educating to having real conversations is imminently powerful.

In my own experience, board members, directors and senior executives are incredibly intelligent people. Regardless of the size of company, industry they operate in, or challenges that their businesses face, each is there to contribute, help, steer, guide and ultimately ensure the business is successful. Clearly, for large organisations, cyber security's impact and implications are equally as large. Boards and executives of these organisations have a wealth of resources under them and therefore are able to ask the right questions, to understand the "why" behind the message and to help steer the ship. However, for smaller organisations without those same resources, cyber security remains just as large a challenge. In some cases the challenge is greater – one incident could completely wipe out the company. Furthermore, cyber security is also an issue that impacts each and every individual person that uses the Internet – from the smallest toddler on an iPad to the grandparent using Skype, Facebook and YouTube to follow the growth and life of that cute little toddler. It is for all these reasons that I am enthusiastic about this book. Anything that can be done to better educate people and better inform decision makers who shape and drive our businesses is a really good thing.

Cyber security can be intimidating. It is too easy to focus on the fear, uncertainty and doubt that this industry loves. The industry is full of jargon and far too much technical speak; a real gift is to be able to break down those barriers and explain the simple things (the 1 percenters) that can be done to make a massive difference. This book is that gift. A cover to cover read will certainly make for an interesting flight – however, I suspect that it will also become quite a good reference book to flick back to. When your "IT guy" sends you a message saying that the email proxy is down and you have just received a spear phishing email, it will be worth quickly flicking open this book and reading those two pages.

The other way that I personally hope people use this book is within the last few pages where the authors have provided some really useful "checklists" to take away, a one page cheat sheet for the tangible things that can be done. Starting with these sheets and next steps will provide people with a really positive way forward. While they are not the silver bullet for cyber security, doing these things will certainly make a massive contribution towards protecting you, your family and your business.

Enjoy this book. I certainly did. And do not hesitate to get a little crazy. Living in the cyber world certainly gets crazier every day, but our lives would not be the same without it.

Troy Braban

Acknowledgment

Troy has been, and continues to be, a brilliant sponsor of things he believes in. With cyber security awareness to directors and the general community, I have been very fortunate to be caught in the cross hairs of that support. Troy is a rare breed and someone I admire, trust and respect, as does the industry and community.

Troy is passionate about people, leadership and building great teams. He is a strategy and change leader and has worked in senior roles in the finance, telecommunications, government and entertainment industries. He also worked in the consulting industry for many years and has experience in delivering large transformation programs. Troy was one of the founding members of the Australian IT Security Expert Advisory Group for the Critical Infrastructure Advisory Council on Australia's National Critical Infrastructure.

Troy won the 2014 AusCert / SC Magazine Australian CISO of the Year and being part of his team was voted the best place to work at the AISA National Conference 2014.

As you will see in the course of this book, everyone and every organisation owner or director needs a 'cyber security peer'. Therefore, I feel very privileged that Troy has provided this foreword to **Gotcha!**.

Dr. Sally Ernst

Contents

Foreword 5
Acknowledgment 9

CHAPTER 1: We're all a dot com 15
   The Gotcha 21

CHAPTER 2: Some scenarios … 25
   Scenario 1: APT and Destructive Payload 26
   Scenario 2: Supply Chain Risk 28
   Scenario 3: Medical Centres 30
   Scenario 4: The Horse has Bolted 31

CHAPTER 3: How Things Work (and do not Work) 35
   The Internet 36
   Servers and the Cloud 38
   Corporate Networks 40
   Firewalls 42
   Antivirus 45
   VPNs 46
   Encryption 47
   Passwords 48

CHAPTER 4: Additional Prevention Measures 51
   Protecting the 'Endpoint' 52
   Monitoring 54
   Well-tested Incident Response Plans 56
   Knowing our Vulnerabilities 56

  Backups 57
  Strategic Cyber-security Governance 58
  APT and Government Contact 59

CHAPTER 5: Some Terms We May Have Heard 63
  Big Data 64
  Botnet 64
  BYOD 65
  Cookies 65
  Distributed Denial of Service Attack 66
  Drive-by 67
  Waterholing 67
  External Media 68
  Insiders 68
  Phishing 69
  Spearphishing 71
  Ransomware 71
  Remote Access Tool 72
  Social Media Leakage 72
  Spyware 73
  Viruses, Worms and Trojans 74
  Blended Threats 75

CHAPTER 6: What to Do Next 77
  For everyone 78
  For Small to Medium Businesses 81
  For Larger Government or Corporations 85

CHAPTER 7: CyberBasics Checklists 91
  Checklist for Everyone 92
  Checklist for Small and Medium Business 95
  Checklist for Larger Government or Corporations ... 98

End Notes	103
The Card Game	110
About the Consulting Editor	111
About the Author	112
About Gotcha!	113

CHAPTER 1

We're all a dot com ...

Everyone is now working in an IT company, and we are ever-increasingly interconnected. As a result, we are also ever-increasingly vulnerable. There is no silver bullet for cyber security. It is all about risk management and, more than ever before, it is about understanding the importance of IT in-house, throughout our supply chain, and within our ecosystem.

Cyber security can be difficult to understand, like everything business and in law; however, ignorance is no excuse. Board directors and key executives are still the ultimate owners of this risk. "Go talk to IT" just does not cut it anymore.

The good news is that much of the knowledge for changing behaviour, and many of the products and services, exist in the public domain to help prevent, detect, and manage cyber security risks.

The need now is to engage people, including board directors and business owners, in cyber security. In order to overcome barriers to this engagement, we need to be empowered with knowledge, have places to turn to, and embed cyber security to be relevant to our walk of life and role in the organisation.[2]

Very high net worth individuals, board directors, and senior executives of very large businesses, may be thinking:

> *"I've thrown all these resources and budget at the cyber security problem only to find out there's malware on my system. How do I justify further spending?"*

> *"What should I be purchasing to best address the cyber security risk to my business?"*

> *"Should I even bother trying to get on top of this problem?"*

> *"What of the marketing hype? Who should I trust for security products and services?"*

> *"How do I distinguish between fact and scaremongering?"*

> *"How much are my competitors spending on this problem?"*

> *"I spend all this money; why have we never picked up a single incident?"*

Directors, entrepreneurs and senior executives of small to medium sized businesses may be thinking:

> *"Well if government agencies and large businesses are being breached, what hope do I have of making my business more secure with limited knowledge and resources?"*

> *"My business does not have anything of value to an attacker.... does it?"*

As individuals, we may be thinking:

> *"How can I protect myself, my workplace, my family?"*

> *"Where do I even start? Who do I turn to?"*

> *"But I'm not wealthy!"*

"Organisations protect the money and personal information I have with them, don't they?"

We can see in the mainstream media every day that the issue of cyber security is affecting us all - from the boardroom to the office to the home.

The key is to be aware of the problem, why and how it is happening, and use this information to identify and manage business and personal cyber security risk. In today's environment it is prudent to assume we have been, or will be, breached.[3] In many cases we just may not realise it.[4]

Cyber weapons are being used with state resources directly to attack foreign citizens and organisations. They have also proliferated freely on the internet such that other organisations and individuals with scarce resources can also hire or use cyber weapons to similar effect.

It's important, then, to be less concerned with governments, organisations and individuals that have our best interests at heart - and more concerned with those that do not, yet have similar capabilities.

Cyber security risks are driven by a number of attacker profiles and objectives:

1. **Nation States,** where a government's cyber weaponry is used to give advantage to its own citizens and/or disadvantage citizens of foreign countries.

2. **Organised criminals,** who may be primarily after money, achieve their objective by stealing information to sell on the black market and 'kidnapping' information for ransom.

They may also be after personal information, identities and computing resources (botnets), which can be used directly or as part of targeted attacks on other high value individuals and businesses.

3. **Hacktivists,** who are activists with cyber capability that purport to be doing a social good by harming us and/or our organisations in retaliation for some perceived wrongdoing to society. They may do anything from corrupting information or disrupting productivity to destroying information.

4. **Terrorists** are active in the cyber domain and increasingly follow physical attacks with waves of cyber attacks. They may also recruit, communicate and influence using and 'hijacking' social media.

5. **Businesses and industry** may also engage in activities like espionage, even targeting smaller businesses. Their objective is likely commercial gain through stealing information such as intellectual property, research and development, pricing, mergers and acquisitions information. Their objective may also be to disrupt productivity and impact reputation.

6. **Individuals,** such as disgruntled and former employees, can represent an 'insider threat' to the organisation. There are also those individuals that may not be overtly malicious, such as an employee who makes an error or a 'script kiddy' that has just learned a new - freely available with help guides - method or tool for hacking. The outcome, however, for the individual or business affected may be just as painful.

7. **State-sponsored actors** hacktivists or organized criminals who are unofficially sponsored by nation state resources in order to aid with deniability. Where industry is closely integrated with the state, those resources may be officially available to them.

The Gotcha

While not the whole story, attacks are often initiated by delivering malware direct to our machines and devices through things like phishing, drive-bys and external media.

 An email that looks legitimate, but when a link or attachment is clicked on, malware may run.

 A website that looks legitimate, but when visited, malware may run.

 **Inserting a USB, charger, mobile CD, or DVD that is infected, and may come from the manufacturer already compromised.**

The 'gotcha' is that these methods can bypass traditional protections, including antivirus, firewalls, VPNs, encryption, strong passwords, and perimeter security.

Once on our machines or devices, the attacker may have, or be able to gain, sufficient access to do and see on our machines or devices what we can do and see. This includes other systems to which we have access in order to achieve their wider objectives.

The good news is there are ways the 'gotcha' risks can be managed. While technology is important, much of the way we can address the problem is based on collective good governance and practices. Some of these good practices are summed up along with checklists at the end of this book.

First, let's take a look at some illustrative scenarios.

CHAPTER 2

Some scenarios ...

The following are publically available scenarios from the mainstream media illustrating cyber security risks and their consequences for us and our businesses.

Scenario 1: APT and Destructive Payload
Online search terms: Shamoon, Wiper, Saudi Aramco, Sony[5]

Sony was not the first business reported to be hit with a destructive attack.

In August, 2012, a large-scale cyber attack at Saudi Aramco reportedly rendered just under 30,000 machines inoperable and stole and destroyed their information, using the "Shamoon" worm.

Reports describe that the entire network and email had to be disabled to stop the infection spreading, and that it took Saudi Aramco two weeks to fully restore its functioning. There was still disruption reported for months later.

The destructive component of Shamoon is "Wiper", functionally common to a number of viruses, including that used in the attack on Sony. Wiper does what it says on the tin – wipes all data, indeed very securely deletes it, including the information a computer needs to start up.

The malware could have initially been delivered via an insider, external media, a direct or indirect phishing attack, a driveby attack, or some combination. As a worm, only one machine needed to become infected for the malware to spread to servers and other machines connected to it - and those to others - without any further human intervention.

Saudi Aramco's business is part of Saudi Arabia's national infrastructure and harming them could harm the economy. Therefore, it may have been a state or state-sponsored attack.

However, any individual, business or country could be at risk of a similar attack. Shamoon and similar malware are not particularly sophisticated; they come with help guides for attackers, and are freely available on the internet.

Scenario 2: Supply Chain Risk

Online search terms: Target CEO (also held chairman of the board and president roles) and CIO lost jobs over cyber attack, entry point Target HVAC supplier.[6]

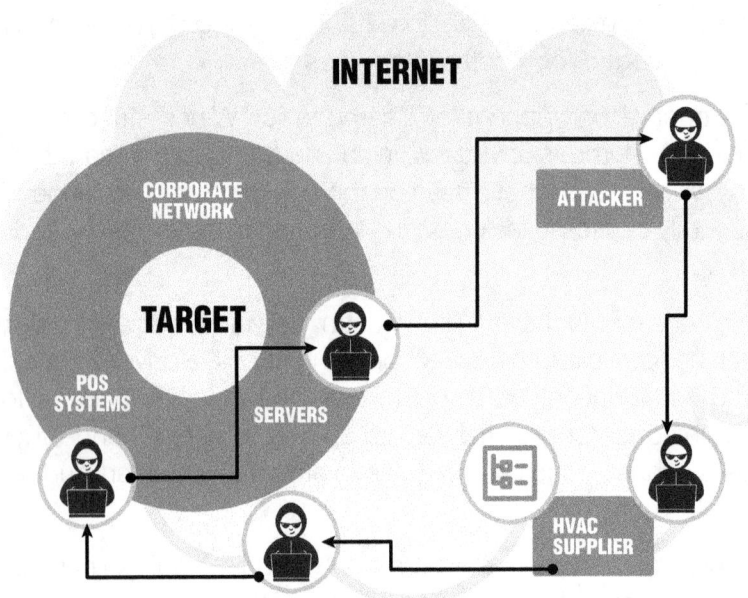

In late November/early December, 2013, Target was the victim of what was reported to be the largest cyber attack in US history at the time.

The attack reportedly affected over 1700 stores with the personal information of over 70 million customers and the details of over 40 million credit cards stolen.

According to reports, the attackers initiated the breach indirectly via Target's air conditioning (HVAC) supplier. With the supplier's credentials, the attackers were reportedly able to gain access to Target's POS systems. While monitoring systems generated alerts, they were reportedly not responded to and Target reportedly only became aware of the attack after the Department of Justice notified them in mid-December.

Lawsuits have reportedly been filed against the company by banks and customers, costs of responding to the breach reached over US $61m, profits decreased 46% from the same holiday period a year before, and the chairman, also holding CEO and president roles, resigned.

There have been similar retailer scenarios in the media from Kmart to Home Depot. Note, however, that this can happen to small businesses too.

Online search terms: credit card information of over 30,000 Australians.

Australian media reported that a ring, broken up by Australian and Romanian national police, managed to steal the credit card information of over 30,000 Australians by hacking the POS systems of Australian small businesses.

We can see, then, that a large company can be compromised by a party in its ecosystem and any business is important in the aggregate, even if it is small.

Scenario 3: Medical Centres
Online search terms: Australian medical centres in ransomware attack.[7]

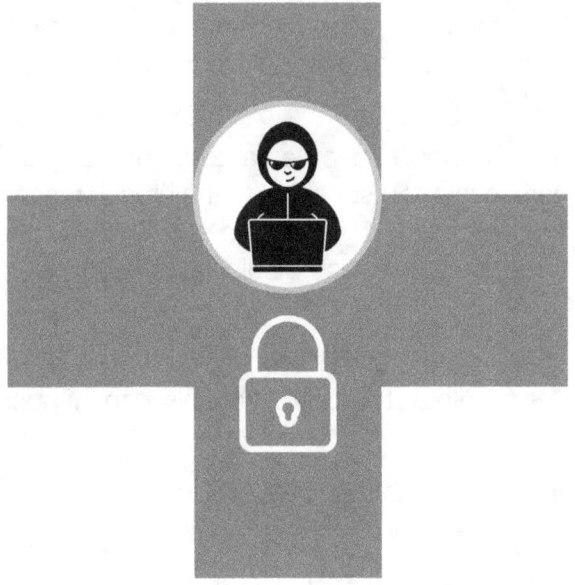

In late 2012, a number of Gold Coast medical centres reportedly fell victim to ransomware attacks. It was not just medical centres, however, and the problem of ransomware continues to this day.

In one publicised case, reports describe how the attackers were able to get past a medical centre's firewall, server passwords, antivirus and into the server holding patient records. All the attacker needed was a phishing email to get in and some tweaked malware that the antivirus had not seen before to get past it.

Once inside, the attackers ran encryption software that blocked access to over seven years of patient records. This rendered the records inaccessible to doctors and medical centre staff, but accessible to the attackers.

Likely organised criminals, the attackers reportedly demanded AU $4,000 to unlock the records and make them accessible. The medical centre reportedly engaged a contractor to try to decrypt files, which proved too difficult. Finally the records were reportedly recovered for the most part from an old offline backup.

In ransomware attacks, organised criminals choose an amount that is cheaper than trying to remedy the problem. Ransoms paid, however, may not return the data and are often followed up with further demands.

This attack, along with the previous scenarios, demonstrate that all businesses face risks no matter their size, and they can put other businesses and individuals at risk too.

Scenario 4: The Horse has Bolted
Online search terms: Gmail hack, iCloud hack.[8]

USERNAME
PASSWORD

Sometimes it may look as if a provider has been compromised when actually it is simply data aggregated from prior attacks to use as 'legitimate' credentials on other systems and services.

In 2014, some high profile attacks were reported from the publication of five million Gmail credentials on a foreign black market forum to Australian iCloud accounts being locked off. Were these actually direct compromises of iCloud and Gmail?

No they were not. These were login credentials gleaned from attacks on other systems and providers, perhaps combined with phishing attacks to verify or learn credentials, and posted to black market forums. The reason it appeared they were compromised was that people had used the same ID and password across multiple systems and/or clicked through on links in phishing emails and given their credentials to bogus sites that captured them. While nonetheless a victim, unfortunately people had, in effect, compromised themselves.

Now that we have some background on the nature of cyber attacks with some illustrative examples of their consequences, let us take a look at how the internet works and how some traditional cyber security methods do and do not work in protecting our information online.

CHAPTER 3

How Things Work (and do not Work)

THE PUBLIC INTERNET

The Internet

The internet is an international, public network, accessible by anyone at any point. Unless otherwise protected, anything sent over or stored directly or indirectly against the internet is like a postcard.

The internet cuts the postcard up into smaller pieces that are publicly identified, labelled and numbered as:

- **Postcard type** (e.g. in internet terms, an email, document, or website)
- **From** (the sender's IP address, which shows where they are on the internet)
- **To** (the recipient's IP address, which shows where they are on the internet)
- **When** it was sent
- **What** order the postcard should be stuck back together in at the other end

Anyone can see this labelling no matter what security is put around it. It is called 'metadata' and helps attackers understand patterns to better target their victims. It also helps forensic experts to identify attackers in a breach.

The postcard then travels through various postal hubs (hops) around the web, internationally, to reach its intended destination. If one hub is unavailable, it will redirect it to another hub to try to get it to the recipient. Anyone can see, copy, change or destroy the postcard along the way.

These postal hubs are generally run by servers that receive, store, and share information (and infections) with each other and with machines and devices. Servers are a gold mine for us, our organisations... and for attackers. The greater the number of people and systems accessing a server, the exponentially greater the risk of infections happening and spreading.

ATTACKER NETWORKS

THE PUBLIC INTERNET

WEBSITES

ATTACKERS

CORPORATE NETWORKS

CLOUD SERVICE PROVIDERS

INDIVIDUAL USERS

HOME NETWORKS

Servers and the Cloud

The 'Cloud' uses the internet and servers to aggregate resources for storing, processing and transacting information. Each virtual server on any physical server may be owned by the same or different people or companies. That is, we may be sharing our physical server or servers with other people and companies in multiple locations.

Generally, with a cloud service provider, but not always, we or our company rents or subscribes to a share of some combination of its resources as a service. That is, generally we do not own or manage these resources and; we share them with other people and companies over multiple locations and they are to a greater or lesser extent managed for us.

These resources could include infrastructure (e.g. datacentres, connectivity), computers (e.g. physical servers), software (e.g. virtual servers, operating systems, applications, and databases), or some combination of the above.

Cloud services adoption is exponentially increasing as in many cases it affords greater flexibility, cost effectiveness, and in some cases robustness. The Cloud Provider may well provide better security than the individual or organisation can in-house, and otherwise more cost-effectively.

We therefore need to be pragmatic in weighing our risks - but we do need to understand them. Once we have defined 'Cloud' in our context, some considerations, include:

- **What data** are we storing in the cloud, and how much do we - or does someone else - care about that data?

- Is our data **encrypted** and, if so, where are the encryption keys?
- **Where** is our data held (data sovereignty), and is that compliant with the regulations our company may be subject to?
- **Who has access**, and what is our comfort level with the 1) staff and their access, and 2) government/s that may have lawful access to our data in that location with or without our knowledge?[9]
- What are the **contractual liability** clauses, and would they cover any loss if something goes wrong?
- How would we **operate through a breach** of their systems?
- Do we have **offline backups** of our data in our control, and do we know how and to where we would restore the information?
- **Are our or our organisation's practices more secure than the Cloud Provider's,** including their private corporate network, which manages the back end of the services we are using?

Let us now have a look, then, at how corporate networks interact with the internet and how some security measures do and do not work.

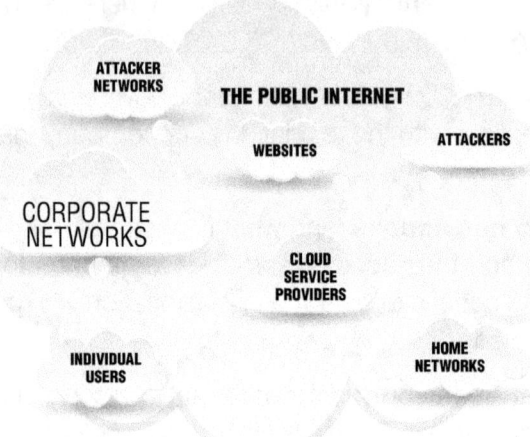

Corporate Networks

There is information within a corporate network that an organisation does not want to be made public, yet it uses a public mechanism to transport and store a subset (hopefully not all) of it.

Within a corporate network there are smaller networks that facilitate internal information sharing. Corporate networks and systems have to differentiate between users as to which have access to what corporate information, and they have to ensure no one else has that access.

A network holding super sensitive information would likely not be connected directly or indirectly to the internet; it would likely be physically separated from the portion of the corporate network that has any direct or indirect access to the internet.

Medium to large organisations may have a De-Militarised Zone (DMZ), which protects the private corporate network from the public internet - like a gate and air gap to an office block.

The DMZ controls what traffic from the internet may enter the corporate network and what traffic may flow back out to the internet. In effect, it allows the users of the corporate network to interact over the internet without having to deal directly with it.

The equipment in the DMZ is normally tightly protected, for example, ensuring servers and devices are 'hardened' through things like operating system minimisation. That is, only the parts that needed to run a particular server are installed. This minimises the number of places vulnerabilities can exist and so reduces the 'attack surface'. Individual applications are also 'hardened', including checking things like control panels for appservers have not been exposed.

Firewalls provide the protection between the internet and the corporate network. Give or take a few bells and whistles, there will likely be a firewall between the DMZ and the internet and another firewall between the DMZ and the corporate network.

Firewalls

In home and micro or small business networks, there will likely be a basic firewall that really just acts as a warehouse. All the warehouse does is close some of its 65,000 odd roller doors (ports) and, of those left open, says what type of postcard can get through which roller door.

If something looks like a duck, quacks like a duck, and waddles up to the right roller door (port) for ducks, the firewall will likely assume it is a duck. Therefore, a bad egg can come through with the good ones.

In a DMZ, the firewall will likely also include Deep Packet Inspection. This is like having a team member at each open roller door to have a closer look at the duck. However, if that duck's wing is not showing any noticeable abnormalities, it will not pick up the bomb under it. That is, if the firewall expects a duck, it is still waddling through the right roller door for ducks quacking like a duck, and the firewall has never seen or been told about a duck with a bomb under its wing, it may still call it a duck and let it through. A firewall needs to know what it is looking for.

Home and corporate networks are equally vulnerable to someone walking into the network with a compromised device and connecting it directly to a machine (e.g. charging their phone, plugging in a USB, running a CD or DVD). This will bypass the firewall.

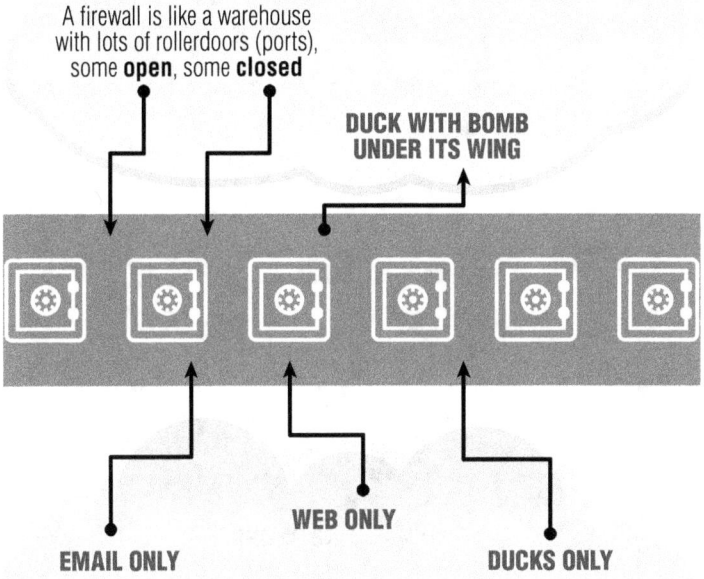

The firewall has to know what it is looking for.

In internet terms, a word document may look legitimate, however, enclosed is a virus (Trojan) that will run when it is opened. It may

have still passed through the firewall because it looked like a word document, had legitimate looking metadata, and went to the right port for file transfer of word documents.

The same applies for any firewall software we may have installed on our machine or device. The virus (malware) that has just made it into our network may affect machines and devices.

Firewalls are still an important part of security, however, and they need to be kept up-to-date.

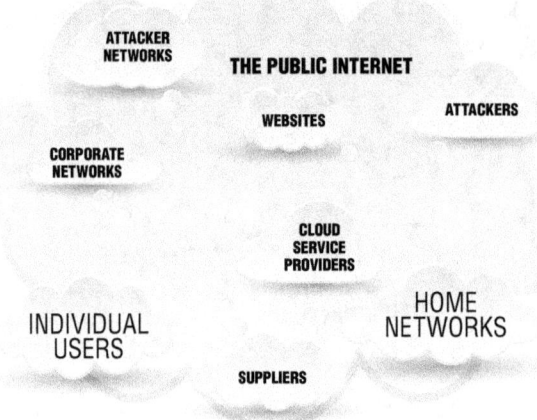

Antivirus

Antivirus provides protection for machines and devices, but it too is not a bulletproof solution.

Think of antivirus like a flu shot, which only protects us from the known strains at the time, i.e.:

- Swine flu vaccine will not protect you from bird flu.
- Last year's flu shot needs to be updated for this year's seasonal strain.
- New viruses have no vaccine until it is discovered and one is developed.
- Some viruses, like HIV, switch off our system's ability to protect us.

Similarly, antivirus software can only stop known viruses and worms. It will not help with new, unknown ones. This is an important point as viruses can be created to change as they spread (Polymorphic Threat). If already infected, your antivirus may be altered by a virus reducing or stopping your protection from other threats, even if known.

Antivirus, like the firewall and other protection measures, can be helpful to protect against malware infections; therefore we need to make sure they are in place and kept up-to-date with patches and latest versions.

VPNs

Machines and devices may also access the corporate network remotely. A VPN may be used to enable this secure remote access as well as intersite communications.

VPNs are password protected. Unless someone has the password and access, no one will be able to easily, if at all, access our data in transit to its destination and if they do, it will be in gobbledygook.

As long, that is, as the attacker does not already have access to our computer. If an attacker can access our computer, they can fire up and log into our VPN client - or watch or take action while we do - and access what we can on our corporate network, doing with that access and data what we can - including propagating infections.

The organisation needs to weigh up, however, the risk of increasing entry points that potentially make it vulnerable with the benefit of remote access for employees and other users. A VPN does, however, make our organisations a harder target than if remote communications were to be allowed unencrypted.

Encryption

Encryption can be used to protect email, voice, chat, documents, and so on. It will secure the contents but not the metadata. Hard drive encryption is important and expected. It can even make files look like they do not exist.

A very strong form of encryption that utilises the principles Public Key Encryption (PKE) is called PGP (Pretty Good Privacy), with an open source version GPG (Gnu Privacy Guard). To explain Public Key Encryption , let's take me - the writer - and you - the reader - as an example. The way it works is that we both have a Public Key known to everyone. Let's call this the 'public padlock'. I take your public padlock, you take mine. I send you something locked with your public padlock (Public Key), so you can access it with your private key and vice versa.

Our private key, however, is stored on a digital key ring on our machine or another device, like a USB, that we will plug into our machine. These private key files are protected with a password.

Assuming we keep our private key safe with a strong password, it is properly implemented, and the underlying cryptography of keys have not been compromised, it is difficult to crack and would take a long time, even with a lot of resources thrown at it.

However, if an attacker has access to our computer, they may gain unfettered access to all the things we have access to, including our encryption keys and passwords. In this case, just as we can unencrypt and see things in postcard form, so can an attacker. They could also delete it.

Passwords

We can see peppered throughout these descriptions that we remain reliant on passwords. Strong passwords may make us a much harder target. However, the issues with passwords are multiple. For starters, as we have discussed before, if an attacker has compromised our machine, they can potentially see or grab our passwords, file contents, and system access privileges. Regardless, passwords for now remain a very important part of cyber security.

Password policies desirably include, at a minimum, 15 mixed-case characters and numbers that are unique for every system used. Once a password is hacked in one place, other internet services using the same credentials also become accessible to the attacker (see Scenario 4).

Where offered, second or multiple factors can be helpful to verify we are authentically us. The second factor needs to be a different type from the first. That is, a password provides something we know. A fob or code, provides something we have. A biometric scan provides something we are, such as a fingerprint. These are three different types of authentication. For 2-factor authentication, we would pick or be offered a method from two different types. It is not a 100% effective solution, but it does make us a more difficult target.

As we can see from this high level overview, we are still vulnerable with risks to be managed. While these traditional cyber security preventions are still important, the next chapter will take us through some additional prevention measures we can consider adopting.

CHAPTER 4

Additional Prevention Measures

Again, many attacks are initiated in a similar way via phishing, drive-bys and external media. These methods seek directly to attack machines and devices using malware.

Falling victim to these methods is primarily a behavioural issue. Therefore, educating and making aware our organisations, supply chains and ecosystems will help to lessen risk. Phishing testing and training is an important part of awareness programs, given this is how most people are compromised.

Protecting the 'Endpoint'

The Australian Signal's Directorate has provided mitigation strategies (ASD Top 4), for which they have won international awards, that if correctly implemented can prevent nominally 85% of these sorts of attacks.[10] To understand the 30ft. view of how these strategies work, let us take a closer look at what malware is.

Malware is:

- prolific
- often not particularly sophisticated, yet still very effective
- freely available on the internet along with help guides and tools for anyone to use against individuals or corporations at the click of a mouse
- traded on professionally run black markets along with guns for hire and names of organisations that are vulnerable

Just like any other software, to be effective malware has to:

1. get onto our machines, and
2. run.

Without running, malware is harmless. Malware does not always require you to click on something to run, some can self-propagate (worm).

The 'ASD top 4' approach mitigates the risks of malware delivered directly to machines and devices through:

1. **Application whitelisting**, which means preventing unauthorised software from running. This may mean the virus cannot run even if it does infect your machine.

2. **Patching applications and operating systems**, which means having the latest software versions and updates (patching) on applications and operating systems. This may mean the malware cannot find the vulnerability it needs to infect our machine. As soon as a patch (software update) is released for a software vulnerability, it is, in effect, a public announcement to attackers to update their tools. They do this within hours and attempt attacks within a day. These attacks can be successful and potentially at scale by the second day. For larger organisations, as a bad patch may wipe out the organisation, a patching regime would include routine and accelerated tasks and staging and testing procedures.

3. **Limiting user privileges**, which means limiting who can do what on a machine to what is needed to perform their role, and particularly restricting administrator privileges.

This may reduce the impact of an attack. An infection while operating in administrator mode, for example, easily gives the attacker our 'keys to the kingdom'. There is also the matter of insider threat.

Where these mitigation strategies cannot be implemented, there are alternative protections called 'compensating controls' that may be used. The key is that we understand the risks associated with this and sign off that we bear them. That is why it is important to have a cyber security peer by our side.

Monitoring

Because it is not bullet proof, the DMZ, and likely the rest of our corporate network, will have monitoring systems in place.

Monitoring systems can be likened to building alarm systems. People wander up to a building and, if the gates and doors are not locked, enter it.

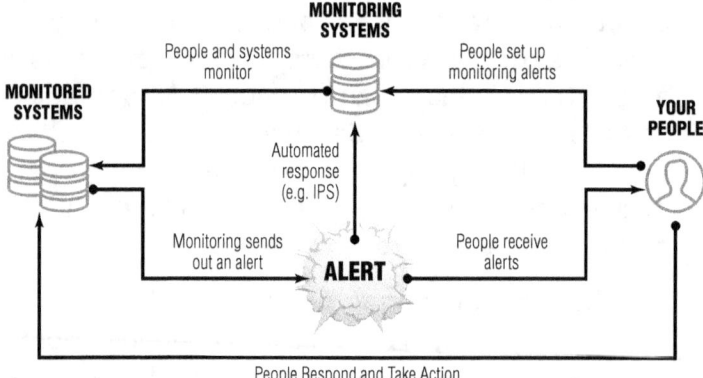

If the alarm system is not on or recording who and what comes in and out of our building, we may not even know someone has been there, who that someone was, or what they did.

If they are already in our building, they can turn our alarm system off so we do not know they are there, find our entry code so they can come in and out undetected, change our entry code so we can not get in, or just destroy or rough up the building and its contents.

If our alarm system sends an alert, we need to act.

The principles are similar in monitoring a corporate network. An Intrusion Prevention System (IPS) may be used for this purpose. An IPS has an Intrusion Detection System (IDS) which monitors activity and, additionally, helps to prevent attacks by blocking them.

An IPS can watch or 'inspect' all activity that passes it across networks and use things it is told (e.g. a duck with a bomb strapped under its wing looks like this) to provide alerts about things happening on the network, machine, or device that may be malicious or suspicious.

An issue is that an IPS can create a lot of alerts and many may be false positives. The expensive part is the analysis of these alerts. An IPS also needs to be updated with new known threats and any changes to the network or devices. It has to know where to look and what it is looking for. Finally, responding to the alerts is critical or the exercise is pointless.

Well-tested Incident Response Plans

If our monitoring systems or our people pick up a problem, we need to know how we will respond. It is important to have a well-tested incident response plan.

The goal is to be resilient to attacks by detecting an incident early, isolating it quickly, continuing to operate through it, and recovering as soon as possible.

Testing defenses is an important part of a protection plan, including engaging in 'blue teaming' this is where defensive 'blue team' team is tested by the 'red team'. During this exercise, they can be assessed on everything from detection of an incident to their incident response capabilities.

Our attackers are not going to give us a heads up that they are about to attack, so we need to ensure this process includes attempts without warning.

Knowing our Vulnerabilities

It is also important to know where our vulnerabilities are. Penetration testing, also known as ethical hacking, is where a team of expert hackers are authorised to try and get into a network. They may, in addition to hacking tools, use social engineering techniques from phishing to walking up to the receptionist to see if they can get an infected USB stick into a machine. This latter, more advanced, social exercise is something that may also be included in red teaming exercises.

Vulnerability-scanning products check what known exploits, and latest software versions and patches, exist in a network. This will

only pick up known exploits, and reports have to be analysed and acted upon for it to be effective.

Compromise assessments may also be performed to assess whether our organisation is under attack and we are just not aware.

Penetration testing, vulnerability scanning, and compromise assessments are only as good as the point in time they were performed, how skilled the testers are, how much integrity they have, and what is done with the information. If recommendations are made and they are not acted upon, the exercise is redundant.

Backups

If an infection occurs or information is changed or destroyed, it is important to be able to wipe the machine and restore from backup. The key issue is what has been backed up....

The problem is threefold once a machine is compromised:

1. **Nothing may have been backed up.** The attacker can compromise backups to make it look like they are being done when they are not. Backups may simply not be performed.

2. **Malware may have been backed up.** Depending on how long it has taken to discover the compromise, malware may have been backed up with data that will then reinstall onto the machines. In the case of cryptographic malware (e.g. ransomware), the backup's data may be locked off too.

3. **Changes may have been backed up.** The backups may have been degraded or an insider may make malicious changes on systems that are then backed up.

Taking frequent backups, timestamping them, and test restoring them helps. The length of time between backups and test restores is a judgement call based on the risk of data loss versus the cost of maintaining valid backups.

Backups need to be kept off-line and in one control.

Strategic Cyber-security Governance

With additional knowledge in-house, and throughout our supply chain and ecosystem, the risk of attack can be better responded to and managed through knowing our data, what of it is important, where it is, and how it is protected.

For a larger organisation, a strategic cyber security peer - someone skilled in both cyber security and organisational governance - is important, along with board member ownership and an executive head of function. They will also help the board and executive better understand the organisation's situational risk, as every organisation's cyber security need is different, even though the initiation or outcome of a breach may be similar.

APT and Government Contact

If an individual or organisation is attacked with state or state-sponsored resources, intent, determination, pressure, and persistence, such an attack is frequently referred to as Advanced Persistent Threat (APT).

APT attackers will literally spend days, and for some hardened defence companies even months, getting at a target organisation directly and through other associated people and organisations, such as their supply chain. They will research all of these stakeholders in great detail and use it to get to the organisation and steal enormous amounts of information over a long period of time - from the organisation, its supply chain, and its employees.

The goal may be to coerce the company or agency into an unfair deal or kill off the target organisation or sector slowly by making them uncompetitive. At the same time the attacker organisation may make significant economic gain through the information they gather and disseminate to companies of relevance in their own country.

The first evidence of the attack may be in lost contracts (lost revenue), loss of negotiating power, cheaper copies of products appearing in the market, and in the returns department (increased costs). This may take a long time to appear and may already be too late.

More recently, there is good cause to fear attackers may destroy organisations or sectors quickly by stealing then wiping data and rendering machines inoperable (Scenario 1).

If an organisation is a victim of APT, the government may make contact (Scenario 2) and if not, it is important for them to be contacted, as and when the attack is uncovered.

If the attack is caught early enough, good forensic information may be found to pursue the attackers, look at adaptive business models, know the attackers' objectives and what they have stolen, and in any case, the threat may be stopped before bringing the organisation down. Security professionals may even be able to turn the attackers' energies against themselves.

If our government contacts us about a breach - engage. These are the good guys that have our best interests at heart and are there to help us. They do not make any money from it and they are not trying to sell us anything.

The important things you can do include:

- **Having a mechanism for the government to get in touch** such as a notifications link on your website in case of a product or media security concern.

- **Verifying the person or people making contact are genuine.** Engage with the contact to establish how to verify they are who they say they are

- **Not recording any details on email.** In the case of APT, the attackers have access to our organisation's email and will be looking for it. We do not want them to know we are onto them.

Our government would not be contacting us if we did not have a very large problem. That said, our organisation will not be their only issue at hand and there will likely be an aggregate of cases we are a part of. The government contact may provide extremely important contextual detail. Specialist firms will then need to be engaged to help.

CHAPTER 5

Some Terms We May Have Heard

Big Data

As any good entrepreneur or agile corporate knows, it is one thing to obtain a lot of information, but it is another to execute on it and exploit it to our advantage. This is where big data technologies come in.

Using big data technologies, domestic and global actors can analyse large amounts of information, derive meaning from it, and disseminate it to the criminals and competitors of most relevance for exploiting it against us, our company and our industry.... perhaps even our country.

Even a seemingly unimportant file on its own can have meaning, and perhaps even significant meaning, in the aggregate.

Botnet

A botnet is a network of machines and devices used to attack other machines and devices. As a botnet is aggregated infrastructure, it is also known as a 'malicious cloud'.

The owners of the machines in a botnet may have been infected with malware and may not be aware their computing resources have been recruited to be a part of it.

With these aggregated computing resources, which can also hide the identity of the true attacker, DDOS attacks and large-scale phishing attacks can be launched. These attacks can disrupt websites and organisations, take them offline, place more malware on more machines and/or steal credentials.

BYOD

BYOD stands for Bring Your Own Device. This is 'the standard' for home and some smaller business networks. That is, there are no standards.

Corporate networks, however, generally do run on standards. The risk associated with BYOD is that they are:

- not owned or controlled by the company
- tend to access higher risk home and public Wi-Fi networks on the road
- generally portable and can wander in and out of the corporate network

It is also important to remember that most devices are also recording devices and could compromise everything from a board room meeting to a by-the-cooler chat to a photo of information on a computer screen.

Cookies

A cookie is simply a storage area in our browser for information about our transactions with a particular website. It may include username and password information, financial or credit card information, shopping cart information, personally identifying information, browsing histories, and so on. We may see requests from time to time pop up in our browser to accept that a site uses cookies, and the site operator's use policy.

Storing this information can help make our browsing experience richer and more convenient. However, the flip-side is the risk of the information falling into the wrong hands. Cookies can be used for good and for bad.

Distributed Denial of Service Attack

In a DDOS attack, our DMZ, webserver, and other internet facing servers may be hit with a flood of internet traffic, which will stop any other traffic getting in.

Even if we are not directly attacked, we may also be affected by another server nearby that is the target of the DDOS attack. To the outside world, it will look like our website or other corporate service is offline.

Think of it like a street protest against a single shop. That street protest can stop all shops in that street from being accessed, not just the shop being targeted. It also slows down any other traffic trying to go through that street to other destinations far and wide and have a knock-on effect to other streets used to go around the protest.[12]

Note that DDOS attacks are sometimes used to distract the organisation and security teams from another more serious attack.

Drive-by

A 'drive-by' is where a person's machine or device picks up a virus just by visiting a website. The person need do nothing more than visit the site - they do not actually have to click on anything. When a website is requested, all information is downloaded to the machine, including infections.

This is usually an opportunistic attack where vulnerable webservers are compromised, infecting websites that are hosted on them. Any person visiting that infected website whose machine or device is vulnerable to the virus will be infected and may spread the infection.

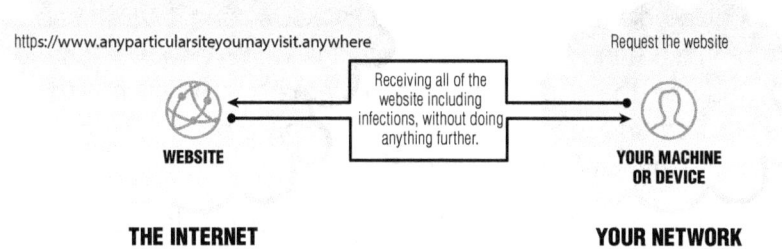

Waterholing

Waterholes are targeted drive-by sites. Here the attacker researches a target or target group to find out the sites they visit in hopes that they have security vulnerabilities. This information may be gleaned from the sector they are in, the black market, or through Social Media Leakage.

The attacker will test for any exploitable vulnerabilities in the webservers hosting these websites. They will then exploit those vulnerabilities to infect the server with malware that will be automatically downloaded to the targets' machine or device when they visit it and infect them if they are vulnerable. It can also potentially infect other visitors' machines if the attacker is not as sophisticated in only infecting machines coming from their chosen victim's IP range.

External Media

External media, such as USB sticks, CDs, and DVDs, can be compromised and then infect a machine with malware if inserted. This may be the case even if the external media is unused and straight from the manufacturer as it may have been compromised during the manufacturing process.

This also applies to connecting to other people's devices such as sharing, bluetooth, Wi-Fi, and charging phones and other devices on computers.

External media may be used by insiders to compromise a network.

Insiders

A person with physical access to our machine or device can also compromise it. They may do it with non-malicious intent, as in an

error or unknowingly using infected external media or network access, or with malicious intent.

Whether an employee, a visitor, a friend, our son downloading music, our daughter downloading movies, or a cloud provider through their back end systems, insiders represent a threat to our systems if they have physical or network access to them.

This is also the case when using seemingly safe practices, such as a VPN or other methods of remote access to view data remotely. If someone can see or view our data, even if it is still sitting on our servers in a different geographical location, there is a risk they can take a photo or screenshot of it and steal it.

It is important to be aware that the more trust someone has in our networks, the greater the vulnerability they represent. This includes our system administrators and security professionals.

Phishing

At its most basic, phishing targets a common vulnerability in machines, devices and people - not a person or group specifically (see spearphishing for targeted attacks).

The attacker will use an email list that is bought, scraped from corporate websites, social media, and/or stolen from other companies' databases in other phishing or hacking attacks.

Likely using a botnet for resources and to cover their tracks, at the click of a mouse the attacker emails a virus enclosed in an attachment or website link to this list. Any machine or device that

is vulnerable to the type of virus may be infected if the malicious attachment is opened or link clicked on. Any of the machines and servers connected to the infected machines could then catch the infection if they are vulnerable. In the case of clicking through on a link, credentials may also be provided to a bogus site that are then stolen by the attacker.

The email may look legitimate and we may just open it because we think it really is from someone, or about something, we care about. There is, however, likely something in the malicious email that does not 'look and feel' right from logos and branding, to grammar, expression, and spelling.

The sender of a malicious email may make it look like a common, trusted organisation such as a social media site, a government agency, or a bank. The problem here is two-fold: the attackers are affecting a legitimate company by closing down a communications channel when IT departments tell people to delete emails from that brand. The other problem is that by not giving this advice, IT departments risk people clicking on malicious links and attachments that are being sent imitating those brands.

Whenever there is a high profile media event, from celebrity weddings and funerals to bombing attacks to tsunami appeals, malware will follow. People often pass around false and malicious emails based on these events, instead of going directly to trusted sources. This propagates the malware through machines, devices, and organisations.

Spearphishing

Spearphishing is a targeted attack on an individual or group. In this type of attack, the individual or individuals who are being targeted are researched through Social Media Leakage. This will make the email more likely to be trusted by the target. Targeted attacks may also use indirect means, such as compromising people the target associates or works with, as a stepping stone to accessing the true target's machine or device and to finding out personal interests to target less secure sites the target visits, such as a local school or sports website (drive by).

Ransomware

Attackers use ransomeware to encrypt data and potentially steal it at the same time (Scenario 3). They then demand a ransom for the encryption key.

Normally using a phishing attack, the attacker delivers cryptographic malware, such as a cryptolocker, that encrypts the victim's information so it cannot be accessed. A pop-up window may appear, as in spyware, to demand a ransom for restoring access. Before doing this, though, they may degrade backups or make it look like backups are happening when they are not.

Scareware looks like ransomware. This is where an attacker may make threats in a pop-up window that are purely blackmail. The machine needs to be cleaned immediately; not a fine paid.

Remote Access Tool

Remote Access Tools (RATs) can be a helpful "back door" to our devices and other machines. Remote Access Tools have legitimate uses for remotely accessing services and our machines for administration, such as tech support.

However, RATs can also be used by attackers in the same way for malicious purposes. They allow the attackers to do and see exactly what we can do and see on our machine – right down to deleting all our data, turning our antivirus off and listening in on webcams and microphones. RATs can even send SMS alerts letting the attacker know when a machine comes online. Once an insider, attackers can silently spread these helpful backdoors all over our network.

Social Media Leakage

Social Media in the online sense is usually looked at as a way to connect and communicate with many people, and more often we hear the term Social Media Marketing. However, Social Media is also a gift for attackers.

We are increasingly publically displaying who we are, who we are connected to, how we are connected to them, what we like and dislike, what is new and old, and what is of interest to us. Attackers are using this valuable information to better target us. The consequences can extend to the grooming of children, romance scams, and the physical loss of property.

Social Media Leakage can provide information through things like social media posts, videos and 'likes', press releases, job ads, 'about us' information on websites, and dating sites.

Information stolen from other compromised machines and data may be pieced together with big data technologies, along with these other social media channels.

Spyware

Spyware programs can run silently without our knowledge on our machine, devices, and through our browsers.

There is a legitimate use for spyware in browsing where we may agree to allow a business to track us, for example through cookies, key search terms, or keyword searches in emails. In return we receive something of value such as more relevant advertising results, free email services, or a better browsing experience.

Spyware allows attackers to watch what we are doing on our machine as well as steal information, including passwords, and may use keyloggers that record what we type on our keyboards.

Attackers using spyware can do things like:

- change browser and machine configurations, that may make them slow or throw up unwanted ads or ransom demands.
- create new users on machines, which allow them to access other systems, such as those of suppliers, customers, partners or home networks.

If targeted, attackers may start with an initial infection to download more malware that can do more damage to our machines, access other machines, and/or steal more things.

Viruses, Worms and Trojans

At the highest level, a computer virus, just like a biological one, requires human interaction to spread. A Worm is like an advanced virus in that it does not require any further human interaction to spread. A Trojan is the legitimate-looking 'packaging' they are delivered in, such as a word document or pdf.

To unpack this high level understanding, a virus requires human contact to spread. For example, a human sends an email with an infected link or attachment. Another human opens that attachment and their computer becomes infected. For it to spread from there, that human has to include the infected attachment or provide the link in another email, and another human has to open it and so on.

A worm does not need human interaction to spread; it tunnels through computer systems and networks independently, similarly to how a live worm tunnels independently through wood or the ground. A worm can be thought of as an advanced virus. Like a virus, which runs a malicious set of code, a worm's code additionally includes instructions to replicate itself onto other vulnerable machines.

The effect of the virus or worm (malicious payload) can range from nil to destructive, again, just like a biological one, depending on what it is designed to do. It may do anything from corrupt to delete files, take over our machine's resources to use as part of a grid or

army of computing power to use in attacks against others (botnet), alter the functioning of the machine, and even stop it functioning.

Blended Threats

An attacker may come into a network through a phishing or driveby attack or as an insider with external media or privileged rights to access systems and information.

The outcome of all of these mechanisms is that the attacker becomes an insider, if they are not already one, and sits on your corporate network bypassing all other cyber security measures.

The attacker's goal is to increase what they can see and do through a network and those it is interconnected with to insert back doors, place wipers or other malicious activity to steal, and destroy or degrade your and others' data over time.

While they are doing these things, they may distract with something like a DDOS attack so resources are focussed on that obvious problem at hand, diverting them from the more serious compromise that may be happening in the network.

Whether an individual, a small business, a large corporate or a government agency, attacks are generally initiated in the same way, regardless of the desired outcome, and can have the same devastating impact. It boils down to good practices across the board and the time, cost, and effort we are willing to put in versus the attacker.

CHAPTER 6

What to Do Next

It is not all doom and gloom. We depend on the innovations that the internet enables, and is enabling, and we want to take advantage of it. This book is not meant to stop us and, again, it is not the whole story. The purpose is to provide some basic understanding of cyber security and empower us to ask the right questions, engage in good practices, and better manage its risks.

We want to take advantage of the reach, productivity, and functionality of the internet to maximise our own and/or shareholder value. We also want to use it much less insecurely to reduce the risk of the opposite happening and the potential of wiping out ourselves, our organisations, and others. Approaches to cyber security need to balance these risks in context.

In this chapter and the appended checklists, there are some basic things we can do to protect ourselves and our organisations. Putting some of these basics of good cyber security practice in place can make us and our organisations a much harder target and disrupt the current market stronghold the attackers are enjoying.

For everyone

1. **Be wary of strange emails and do not send them on**. We should never click on links in emails we do not recognise. For ones we think we do recognise, we can 'hover' to check the true URL. We can also go straight to the source, rather than clicking through.

2. **Use unfamiliar secret question/answers** instead of real ones. In many cases the attackers can find our

date of birth, mother's maiden name, high school, first boyfriend/girlfriend and pet's name via social media or other records. Using made-up answers means that even if they find that information they cannot use it against us. We just need to make sure the 'made up answer' is something we can remember!

3. **Think before posting**. We need to be careful about what information we put online about ourselves, our families, and our workplaces. Online we may also be advertising the things we like and dislike, which may also be used against us by untrusted sources and attackers. We need to verify who and what we are connecting to.

4. **Protect personal computers and devices**. Local technology shops can help with what we need to do and how to keep software up to date, including routers, firewalls, applications and soon your 'things' like smart meters, home automation systems … fridges …toasters ..etc.

5. **Use strong passwords when needed, make them unique to each important online service, and enable 2-factor authentication where offered**. We need to use a unique, strong password to access our internet banking, for example. However, to access something non-sensitive, like a regularly used news app, then something simple and easy to remember could be considered. Unless, that is, we are storing our credit card in the app – then it needs to be secure. Enabling 2-factor authentication helps make us a much harder target. It is a good idea to enable it where offered.

6. **Keep offline backups of important information**, and it is important these backups are in our control even for information stored with cloud or external service providers. This may be on a USB stick, hard drive, CD/DVD or similar. Testing whether the data is available is important too because attackers can make it look like our data has backed up even when it has not. By time-stamping these backups we may be able to restore from the last known good backup, prior to infection.

7. **Try not to share external media**; this includes charging mobile phones on other's machines and sharing USB sticks, external hard drives, and CD/DVDs.

8. **Do not download untrusted software**, including pirated movies, music and modifications to programs not provided by the trusted source. These are often infected and make our networks vulnerable. If we then go back into corporate or other networks, physically or via our technology, with infected devices, we are also putting our organisation in addition to friends, family and acquaintances at risk.

9. **Make cyber security a 'dinner table' conversation**. The more of our friends and family we can make aware, the less vulnerable not only they become, but also we and our organisations become. Attackers look for both direct and non-direct routes to get to their target. The very social interconnectivity and reach that we enjoy, attackers use against us.

10. **Be aware of the 'offline' consequences of cyber incidents.** An attacker with information obtained online may also use it to cause harm and defraud us via phone or 'snail mail'. For example, we need to be aware of people calling us from our bank or sending through the post winning tickets that require more information from us. We can check the source and call back to a publicly advertised and trusted number, which may not necessarily be the one they gave you. Attackers may also groom children online to meet offline or to divulge information or pictures. Romance scams may also be initiated this way to ultimately defraud.

For Small to Medium Businesses

Small to medium businesses do not have massive resources, a large security team to call upon, or large amounts of money to spend on cyber security. However, ignoring cyber security activities can be dangerous, as highlighted throughout this book. Here are some tangible things that every small or medium business should consider.

1. **Get educated.** Reading this book is a brilliant start. Now we know what cyber security is.

2. **Educate people, and encourage them to do the same at home.** As a people problem, it is useless if we are well informed but everyone in our business is not. Continually provide reminders and advice about what employees

should be doing to protect themselves, customers, their family and friends, and the business.

3. **Know what the business has of value in-house and in its ecosystem.** Even smaller organisations may be holding credit card information, patient records, financial information, or have access to, or hold information for, a more targeted organisation. As we can see from the scenarios and information in this book – this makes the business a higher value target and increases its risks and obligations from a cyber security perspective.

4. **Get some help.** We can be creative and innovative for how to get some help. Smaller businesses cannot afford a top tier consulting company and nor should it have to. However, here are some creative ideas for accessing low cost assistance:

    - Contact a local university. There may be an industry work experience scheme the business could participate in or graduates that are keen for some experience by helping out a day a week.

    - Contact a local cyber security industry body. Many of these bodies have a large member base of passionate security professionals. Some will be willing to work "on the side", some will happily "volunteer", and others will be currently out of work and looking for an opportunity to do something useful. There is the added bonus of having the industry body 'reference check' the person through their own experienced network.

- Contact a large supplier. They may lend their business's expertise and capabilities as they, too, are only as secure as their weakest link.

5. **Get the business's online world in order.** The business needs to have a **privacy** policy and protect its **customer data**, from customer or patient records to financial information, such as credit cards. It also needs to ensure **credit cards** are not being accepted by insecure email and are kept secured with a **PCI compliant** provider and is otherwise PCI compliant. Ensure the business's website uses a secure certificate to protect its customers.

6. **Protect all business computers and devices** All of the business's computers and network need to have things like an up-to-date firewall, router, applications and anti virus capability. This does not need to be expensive. Try to keep work machines separate from personal and social uses.

7. **Keep software up-to-date** with the latest operating system (e.g. Windows, Mac) and versions for any software, including third party applications (e.g. Office, Java, Adobe, Flash.) The one thing that smaller companies can do much more easily than bigger ones is update to the latest operating system and versions for any software, including third party applications, and patch... patch ... patch.... That is, keep them updated on an ongoing basis. As the business gets larger, it will need to put in place a robust patching regime (see Checklist for Larger Organisation).

8. **Hold offline backups of important information.** Even if the business is using a cloud service provider, it is important to have an offline backup in its control that is time stamped and test restored. It is also important to know where and how the data would be restored if needed to keep the business operating.

9. **Control the keys to the kingdom.** Whomever runs the network and/or has administrative access to the business's computers, data, backups and websites has privileged access to information, meaning they can potentially do and see anything. It is a question of trust. It is also a judgment call on managing the risk of parting on acrimonious terms and otherwise disgruntlement while still employed.

10. **Do not use machines and devices in 'administrator' mode** unless it is required to perform a task - and then only for that task, such as changing the configuration of a machine or installing new software. The hint with the type of tasks just listed is that if a machine is attacked with malware while in administrator mode, the attacker is easily gaining that sort of access to do those sorts of things too. Instead, create user profiles that provide access, and rights to do things with that access, that reflect the tasks that need to be done.

11. **Be aware of compliance requirements** the business may be subject to 1) in its industry, 2) for the type of data it is holding, and/or 3) for the types of customers it deals with.

12. **Have a cyber security action plan** and track the business's progress on it.

13. **Review the points "For Everyone" above.** Do not click on links in email, use strong passwords, and be careful about what information about the business is placed online.

For Larger Government or Corporations

As a larger organisation, the risks are heightened and attacks may be more targeted. Where we have made ourselves a much harder target, our supply chain and ecosystem may be leveraged to compromise us (see Chapter 3 - APT and Government Contact). Cyber security requires strategic, top-down, decision-making so effective organisational structures can be in place to embed it cross-functionally throughout the organisation, including in any innovation or change.

1. **Board engagement and strategic cyber security governance.** The first thing we need to do is to get educated - a good start has been reading this book. We need to step back and look at our organisation holistically to understand its context, manage risks - including those associated with point or siloed solutions, and maximise cyber security.

2. **Know the data...** the way we know the numbers.
    - A data breach is similar to a breach of our fiduciary responsibility. That is, if we get it wrong, particularly

without having shown due care and understanding, there will be consequences for us, our business, and other stakeholders.

- Similarly to our numbers, for an organisational board director or senior executive it is a structural issue. We need to understand the high level and the factors affecting it, then watch and manage the risks associated with them.

- Like numbers, some data are more important than others, some need to be monitored more closely, some we would not disclose, others we make public, and some are brought together to give core meaning and productivity to the business.

- We need to know what data the organisation has, where it is, what level of importance and sensitivity it has, how it is being looked after, what warning bells are in place, and how they would be responded to.

3. **Engage a cyber security peer.** Have someone on the board who takes ownership for cyber security. The companies where this is the case are almost always better informed and more secure. Similarly, ensure there is a head of function for cyber security, such as a CISO role.

4. **Evaluate situational risk** as every organisation's cyber security need is different, even though the initiation or outcome of a breach may be similar.

5. **Set the policies** and ensure the structures and training are in place for them to be followed and embedded

throughout the organisation, including for any changes and/or innovation. Security needs to be considered ground up.

6. **Educate and make aware the organisation, supply chain, and ecosystem** as technology can only go so far. Much of the risk management today involves adapting behaviour to lessen risk. Our first best line of defence - and vulnerability - is our people and those in our ecosystem. They too need to be educated on cyber security more generally, as well as in the context of the organisation. People will only adopt change if they are engaged or are otherwise forced to comply. Include phishing testing and training in awareness programs - this is how most people are compromised.

7. **Understand compliance requirements.** There may be multiple compliance requirements on the organisation involving cyber security, from contracts to regulations and shareholder value maximisation and reputation protection expectations.

8. **Monitor data and access to it** - and **act on alerts** if something does go wrong. The organisation may require custom monitoring solutions.

9. **Know what to do if something does go wrong.** Have an Incident Response Plan - and **test the plan**. Engage in 'Blue Teaming', where the defensive team is tested by a red teaming exercise, during which they can be assessed on everything from detection of an incident to their incident response capabilities. Our attackers are not going to give us a heads up that they are about to attack, so this process needs to include **attempts without warning.**

10. **Find out where the organisation is vulnerable.** The first step to addressing a problem is identifying it. Engage in penetration testing and vulnerability scanning. Compromise assessments will also help by looking to uncover whether the organisation is already under attack and just unaware.

11. **Hold backups** with offline backups and test restores so if the organisation has to start from ground zero, a valid backup of its information is available and in the organisation's control. Emergency communications and hardware may also be required in a destructive attack.

12. Having a robust **patching regime** (where possible, the latest software versions and updates) that includes routine and accelerated tasks is important, as are staging and testing procedures - a bad patch may wipe out the organisation.

13. **Prevent unauthorised software from running** (application whitelisting).

14. **Limit who can do what on a machine or system** to what is needed to perform their role, particularly system administrator access. Remember, there is no such thing as a 'mover' in your organisation, just 'joiners and leavers'. That is, assess system access needs as people change roles, as well as when they join, ensuring access is removed when they leave.

15. **Multi-layered compensating controls and defences** will likely be required to reduce risk to an acceptable level based on our cyber-peer and security team's advice - and our risk appetite when we sign off on the decisions.[15]

16. **Having a Cyber Security Program** with board reporting, including progress, barriers, and budgeting is essential. Interestingly, cyber security can highlight other governance and management issues in the organisation.

17. **A communications plan** is integral as things can go wrong. Further, board members may be the ones answering for it (see Scenario 2), and sometime incidents may be simply out of our control. A communications plan also incorporates communicating internally and with other organisations and the customers we deal with.

Finally, ensure your supply chain and ecosystem are doing the same.[3]

CHAPTER 7

CyberBasics Checklists

Checklist for Everyone

- ☐ I do not click on links or attachments in emails, texts or messages that do not look right or are from people I do not know.

- ☐ If I am suspicious of an email, text, or message, I contact the person via a different means to verify it.

- ☐ I know what to do if something goes wrong with my cyber security both at home and at work, such as accidently clicking on a malicious link, attachment or message, or if something starts to not look or feel right with my machine, information or devices.

- ☐ If I need to do something on my account online with a service provider, I go directly to their web page to login without going through email or messaging links.

- ☐ I craft secret questions and answers for online identity purposes that are not familiar to avoid identity theft.

- ☐ I think about the consequences before publishing information about myself or others online, and request others do the same.

- ☐ I use separate devices for work and personal use.

- ☐ I verify who or what I am connecting with online.

- ☐ I avoid public wifi, and if I do use it, only non-sensitive information is transmitted.

- ☐ I use strong, unique passwords for important information and service providers, and change default passwords on my home network equipment such as routers.
- ☐ I keep software up-to-date, including, where possible, the latest versions on my own machines and devices.
- ☐ I only use the administrator login on my own machines and devices when necessary and limit what I and my family and friends can do in user profiles limited in access to do what is needed.
- ☐ I password protect all of my devices and they automatically lock if I have not been using them for a period.
- ☐ I never share my login information with others.
- ☐ I backup my important and sensitive information offline, timestamp it, and double check the backup is working and I can restore it.
- ☐ I avoid using, or allowing others to use, external media on my machines and devices, such as charging or connecting mobile phones, USB sticks and CDs/DVDs.
- ☐ I only download software, movies, and music from trusted sources.
- ☐ I have made cyber security a "dinner table" conversation in my household and have my questions and answers prepared.
- ☐ I am aware of the 'offline' consequences of cyber incidents, such as fraudulent phone calls and posted mail, and know

to find an alternative method to verify them before providing any personal or other information.

☐ I know the cyber security policies and procedures my organisation has in place for employees and adhere to them.

☐ I enable 2-factor authentication where it is offered, such as a texted code or one generated by a device I have been provided, to use in addition to my password.

Checklist for Small and Medium Business

- ☐ We stay informed of cyber security risks to our business.
- ☐ We have continuous cyber security education programs, including the Cyber Basics Checklist for Everyone, for our people in-house and encourage our ecosystem to do the same.
- ☐ We know what to do if something goes wrong or there is a cyber incident, including how we would know, keep our business running through it, and how we would recover from it, including an incident response firm already signed up with a Service Level Agreement in place.
- ☐ We regularly review our cyber security in light of changing risks, changes in our organisation and progress we have made in better securing it.
- ☐ We have engaged help for our cyber security needs.
- ☐ We have a CyberMap or list of all hardware and software our business uses and the data that is kept and accessed on, and transmitted using, those systems.
- ☐ We have cyber security good practices embedded in our policies and procedures.
- ☐ We know where our data of high consequence is both in-house and in our ecosystem, including that which sits with employees, suppliers, cloud service providers, and in other networks and devices.

- ☐ We keep our software up-to-date and, where possible, with the latest versions on all operating systems and applications and ensure our ecosystem is doing the same. Where this is not possible or difficult, we have assessed the risk and found alternative ways to reduce it....and we are not running unsupported software like Windows XP.

- ☐ We only provide people with the access to systems that they need to access, and the ability to do what they need to do on those systems, to fulfil their role; where this is difficult, we have put in place alternative strategies to reduce the associated risks to an acceptable level, and we ensure our ecosystem is doing the same.

- ☐ We only allow authorised software to run, preventing all other software from running; where this is difficult, we have put in place alternative protections to reduce our risk to an acceptable level, and we ensure our ecosystem is doing the same.

- ☐ We hold offline backups of important information in our control that are encrypted, time stamped, and test restored.

- ☐ We adhere to our compliance requirements and that of our customers, such as privacy, HIPAA, industry specific requirements, standards, and credit card protection, supported by our policy library that our people are trained on.

- ☐ We have considered specialist cyber security tactical services for systems of high consequence, such as vulnerability scanning, penetration testing, monitoring, and

regular compromise assessments, to reduce our risks to a level acceptable to our organisation.

- ☐ We encrypt information of high consequence at rest and in transit.
- ☐ We enable two or multi-factor authentication on systems that offer it.
- ☐ We have assessed offering two or multi-factor authentication on our systems that we and others use.
- ☐ We know how and who we would communicate with in case of an incident, inclusive of media, customers, government, suppliers, and in-house.
- ☐ We have considered cyber security insurance in the course of our cyber security program.
- ☐ We have reviewed the Checklist for Everyone and understand they are part of our ecosystem, that we are only as strong as our weakest link.

Checklist for Larger Government or Corporations

- ☐ We provide training and briefings to our board members to ensure they are educated and understand the risks.

- ☐ We have a strategic cyber security peer onboard at executive and board level.

- ☐ We have assessed at board/ business owner-level our situational risk, that is, we understand our organisations threat landscape, the likelihood of those threats, and our risk appetite for the magnitude of consequences they could represent to our organisation.

- ☐ We know where our data is and what of it is important, including where it may also live in our ecosystem.

- ☐ We can assure our data is appropriately and effectively protected.

- ☐ We know who has access to our data, what they can do with it, and that those privileges are the minimum required to perform their role including system administrators.

- ☐ We know what technologies are emerging that can help secure our organisational assets and information of high consequence.

- ☐ We evaluate and manage our ecosystem risk as a routine process in our organisation and review it as part of our cyber security program.

- ☐ Cyber security is embedded in all parts of the organisation and including in all policies and procedures.
- ☐ Cyber security is part of our organisation's budgeting process.
- ☐ Cyber security is considered ground-up as part of the organisation's change and innovation processes.
- ☐ We have a comprehensive and timely regime for keeping software up-to-date on all operating systems and applications.
- ☐ We have considered application whitelisting and made an informed decision on its use.
- ☐ We have considered attack simulations commensurate with our threat landscape and tested response plans, without warning, using multiple parties.
- ☐ We have a multi-layer defence plan tested in a cycle appropriate to our situational risk.
- ☐ We have implemented 2-factor authentication on critical systems in-house and in the ecosystem.
- ☐ We have monitoring systems in place with alerts analysed and responded to.
- ☐ We measure how our team would detect a cyber incident, how our organisation would operate through it, and how long it would take to recover from it.

- ☐ We know how and who we would communicate with in case of an incident, inclusive of media, customers, government, suppliers and in-house.

- ☐ We hold offline backups in our control that are timestamped, encrypted and include a test restore procedure.

- ☐ Our information assets and high consequence information are encrypted at rest and in transit.

- ☐ We have an organisational and ecosystem education program for cyber security awareness and adherence to our organisation's policies and procedures that protect it.

- ☐ We are engaged with specialist cyber security firms for tactical services on critical systems.

- ☐ We have multilayered compensating controls on legacy and vulnerable systems.

- ☐ We have a way for the government to contact us in the case of APT.

- ☐ We meet our compliance requirements.

- ☐ We have considered cyber security insurance in the course of our cyber security program.

- ☐ We have reviewed the Checklists for Everyone and Small and Medium Business and understand they are part of our ecosystem, that we are only as strong as our weakest link.

End Notes

A number of people have spent a significant amount of time and effort helping me as a director-type skill up in the area of cyber security and ultimately writing this book.

There have also been so many people benevolent with their intellect in the effort to bring this book to bear and make a positive difference to our community.

Reflecting cyber security as a team sport, these people span cyber security professionals, business owners and directors of organisations of many sizes. It is one thing to gain cyber security knowledge, it is another to be able to share it in a language business people can consume and have time for.

To all of these people, and you know who you are - thank you.

Dr. Sally Ernst

1. Numerous
   a. Business Growth Fund and Barclays (2014) "BGF and Barclays Entrepreneurs Index", UK: https://wealth.barclays.com/content/dam/bwpublic/global/documents/wealth_management/entrepreneurs-index-4-updated.pdf
   b. Ernst, S.A (2009) "EO Investec Entrepreneur Indicator", UK
   c. Ernst, S.A (2010) "EO Global Entrepreneur Indicator", in partnership with Standard Chartered, US
2. Ernst, S., Refiti, L (2014) "CyberInsight: Board Directors and Cyber Security Engagement" Report and presentation at AISA National Conference 2014 Melbourne 17th October, 2014.
3. AFR: http://www.afr.com/p/technology/seven_things_every_director_should_EuV9RhAey0pjzbW20lpMgK
4. Sample article, KrebsonSecurity: http://krebsonsecurity.com/2014/08/dq-breach-hq-says-no-but-would-it-know/
5. Scenario 1 Sample articles from search terms
   a. BBC: http://www.bbc.com/news/technology-19293797
   b. NYTimes: http://www.nytimes.com/2012/10/24/business/global/cyberattack-on-saudi-oil-firm-disquiets-us.html?pagewanted=all&_r=0

    c. SCMagazine:
       http://www.scmagazine.com/making-sense-of-middle-east-targeted-malware/article/266180/

    d. TheRegister:
       http://www.theregister.co.uk/2012/12/10/saudi_aramco_shamoon_inquest/

    e. SCMagazine:
       http://www.scmagazine.com/analysis-of-wiper-malware-implicated-in-sony-breach-exposes-shamoon-style-attacks/article/386781/

6. Scenario 2: Sample articles from search terms

    a. Forbes:
       http://www.forbes.com/sites/samanthasharf/2014/08/05/target-shares-tumble-as-retailer-reveals-cost-of-data-breach/

    b. KrebsonSecurity:
       http://krebsonsecurity.com/2014/05/the-target-breach-by-the-numbers/

    c. news.com.au:
       http://www.news.com.au/finance/business/us-target-gregg-steinhafel-fired-for-data-breach/story-fnkgdftz-1226906694399

    d. BBC:
       http://www.bbc.com/news/technology-25681013

    e. ABC: http://abcnews.go.com/Business/big-data-breach-target-learned-lesson/story?id=24124097

    f. CNN: http://money.cnn.com/2014/02/06/technology/security/target-breach-hvac/

    g. ITNews: http://www.itnews.com.au/News/380947,banks-sue-target-over-security-breach.aspx

    h. TheRegister: http://www.theregister.co.uk/2014/03/14/target_failed_to_act_on_security_alerts/

    i. SMH: http://www.smh.com.au/it-pro/security-it/australias-biggest-ever-data-theft-gang-busted-over-credit-card-crime-20121128-2agzy.html

7. Scenario 3: Sample articles from search terms

    a. ABC: http://www.abc.net.au/news/2012-12-10/hackers-target-gold-coast-medical-centre/4418676

    b. ABC: http://www.abc.net.au/news/2014-01-16/australian-pharmacies-targeted-in-ransomware-attacks/5203970

c. SMH:
   http://www.smh.com.au/technology/ransom-racket-hits-brisbane-businesses-20121230-2bxrz.html

d. SCMagazine:
   http://www.scmagazineuk.com/australian-medical-centre-held-by-ransomware-and-4000-demand/article/272076/

e. MJA:
   https://www.mja.com.au/careers/198/3/online-security

f. CERT:
   https://www.cert.gov.au/advisories/ransomware

8. Scenario 4: Sample articles from search terms

   a. LifeHacker.com:
      http://lifehacker.com/5-million-gmail-passwords-leaked-check-yours-now-1632983265

   b. Mashable:
      http://mashable.com/2014/09/10/5-million-gmail-passwords-leak/

   c. CSO:
      http://www.cso.com.au/article/554793/google-says-5m-gmail-password-dump-wasn-t-because-it-hacked/

   d. Forbes:
      http://www.forbes.com/sites/markrogowsky/2014/09/03/the-celeb-hack-has-people-telling-you-to-turn-off-cloud-backup-ignore-them/

   e. TheGuardian:
      http://www.theguardian.com/technology/2014/sep/01/naked-celebrity-hack-icloud-backup-jennifer-lawrence

   f. BBC:
      http://www.bbc.com/news/technology-27588972

9. ASD:
   http://www.asd.gov.au/publications/csocprotect/cloud_computing_security_considerations.htm

10. Adapted from DSD (2013) 'Strategies to mitigate targeted cyber intrusions':
    http://www.dsd.gov.au/infosec/top35mitigationstrategies.htm
    and SAN Institute (2013) "Critical Controls for Effective Cyber Defence":
    http://www.sans.org/critical-security-controls/

11. With thanks to Mark Stanhope

12. Pinchot, G. & Pinchot, E.S. (1978) "Intra-corporate entrepreneurship" Fall 1978:
    http://www.intrapreneur.com/mainpages/history/intracorp.html

13. Ernst, S.A. (2007) The role of the Corporate Entrepreneur in the Radical Innovation Process Macquarie Graduate School of Management Sydney

14. Ernst and Intrabond Capital (2014) as featured in CFO Duties in the Face of Cyber Security

15. Christensen, Clayton:
http://www.claytonchristensen.com/key-concepts/

16. WIth thanks to Colin Renouf

17. With special and general thanks to Ed

The Card Game

About Gotcha! the Card Game

Gotcha! the Card Game was created on a road trip in January, 2015, testing the Community CyberHealth Roadshow concept that, as a people problem, would bring cyber security to the people. I hope by the time of publishing this is happening.

We were travelling somewhere between the Sunshine Coast, QLD and Torquay, VIC with the cardboard bought for the prototype in Nowra, NSW (while enjoying the interesting Museum there), when a very senior executive in a very large organisation said to me during a conversation on addressing cyber security, "Yes, but how do we engage people?"

The 'bee in my bonnet' came up with this card game - **Gotcha!** - based on some principles in the **Gotcha!** book, including the Australian Signals Directorate's award winning Top 4 Mitigation Strategies.

As always I cannot take credit for these ideas. They were, again, suggested to me by people who actually care and I am executing on them as someone who also does. Nothing is achieved in isolation.

Enjoy. We hope it makes a difference.

Dr. Sally Ernst

About the Consulting Editor

Troy Braban

Troy is passionate about people, leadership and building great teams. He is a strategy and change leader and has worked in senior roles in the finance, telecommunications, government and entertainment industries. He also worked in the consulting industry for many years and has experience in delivering large transformation programs. Troy was one of the founding members of the Australian IT Security Expert Advisory Group for the Critical Infrastructure Advisory Council on Australia's National Critical Infrastructure.

Troy won the 2014 AusCert / SC Magazine Australian CISO of the year and being part of his team was voted the best place to work at the AISA National Conference 2014.

About the Author

Dr. Sally Ernst

Dr. Sally Ernst, co-founder UK and Australian Cyber Security Networks (www.CSNs.co), has over 15 years leadership experience in British and Asia-Pacific tech companies. She has held board positions, contributed to government-led forums, and invested in start-ups. Sally's Doctorate, along with her MBA, specialises in tech intrapreneurship in a radical innovation context and she continues to be involved in industry research. An international cyber security strategist and businesswoman, Sally regularly speaks on cyber security from a holistic business, innovation and governance perspective.

About Gotcha!

By Dr. Sally Ernst

Gotcha! is an important handbook on cyber security for business executives. This book not only raises awareness of the serious nature of the cyber security threat in a language business people can understand, it empowers them with practical steps to follow and key questions to ask their IT people and suppliers.

Gotcha! takes a vital step toward bridging the gap between cyber security experts and the influence of the board, executive and management. Through this, a more informed picture of the cyber security problem can be brought together, businesses can make themselves a harder target, and core business services can become more resilient.

www.ingramcontent.com/pod-product-compliance
Lightning Source LLC
LaVergne TN
LVHW011726060526
838200LV00051B/3041